# Peaceful Poetry

## Justin Widener

Copyright © 2023 by Justin Widener

All rights reserved. This book or any portion thereof may not be reproduced or transmitted in any form or manner, electronic or mechanical, including photocopying, recording, or by any information storage or retrieval system, without the express written permission of the copyright owner except for the use of brief quotations in a book review or other noncommercial uses permitted by copyright law.

Printed in the United States of America
Library of Congress Control Number:     2022923028
ISBN:     Softcover                     979-8-88622-862-5
          e-Book                        979-8-88622-863-2
Republished by: PageTurner Press and Media LLC
Publication Date: 04/19/2023

To order copies of this book, contact:
PageTurner Press and Media
Phone: 1-888-447-9651
info@pageturner.us
www.pageturner.us

# Peaceful Poetry

JUSTIN WIDENER

# 52 Sundays

The last chapter ends and the new season begins
Our faith in God remains and grace and mercy wins
52 Sundays a year 313 other days
We need to serve the others in all other ways

52 weeks a year God has given us to use
Use to serve his children even those who still refuse
Sunday to Saturday everyday in between
Every minute every hour everyone that we have seen

Some say leave it in the church inside the four walls
The people are the church and answering all the calls
The church is alive it moves on down the street
The church continues to grow with the walking of all the feet

Whether a paved path before or a dusty old road
He gives us the strength to carry every load
Jesus is not religion he is relationship
He is the love that we feel the wisdom and every tip

Saving of the sick sinners and the lost
The teaching that our Lord has paid the very cost
So what is beyond the 52 Sundays that we live
What can we do to help and heal and give

Keep being the church continue to live the truth
Be that example so non-believers see the proof
We can fill every pew but let's stand in every door
Let's spread the love of Christ just like every Sunday before

# A Man of God

The tide is high the wind is strong
The persecution felt where did you go wrong
Thrown in a prison and stuck in a cell
What do you do in this living hell

Do you feel sorrow or pity yourself
Or do you stand and pull that Bible off the shelf
The storm clouds have come a tornado on site
Where is your heart where is the fight

Do you turn to the world and hope that it'll pass
Or do you listen to the teacher like you would in a class
The walls are closing in the prison door closed
Just listen to God and the answer is exposed

If you have a dream that you have a new start
Listen to his words and open your heart
Faith of a mustard seed you hold in your hand
He will raise you up and help you stand

Fill your heart with the love of the Lord
He will give you the answer and then even more
Joseph and Daniel and David all fought
They listened to the teacher and became a man of God

# A Mother

What is a mother
The person they call Mom
What is her job description
Where does she come from

A superhero at home
A doctor when you fall
A counselor for the lost
A listening ear when you call

When she became a mother
God filled her from his heart
Gave her the strength she needs
And his will from the very start

He said it won't be easy
And there will be many tears
Her body is going to change
But her heart will fill with years

The size of the outside
Is nothing to be concerned
It's the love inside her heart
And the joys that she has earned

Don't forget about your mom
And sacrifices she's made
The love she has for you
Is something that will never fade

# A Name

He sits on the ground on the crowded street
She shelters under stairs and the sound of people's feet
An old man walking bent over in the pain
They are just a few of the thousands that still remain

No one sees them how they used to be
The warriors from the past now suffering endlessly
At a point in life they made the selfless decision
Leave their families behind to go on a greater mission

Fighting in a war that many don't understand
Losing brothers and sisters in a foreign land
Those that are back home can sleep in peace at night
The soldier is the one that's willing to do the fight

Promises that were made continuing to be broke
When will this nation turn their eyes and become woke
Woke to the battle these veterans fight inside
The veterans on the street that no longer can they hide

They aren't looking for a charity
as they hold a coffee cup
They're looking for some help a hand to hold them up
Each one has a name as they are growing older
No longer wearing the uniform they are still an American soldier

This world is a sea with fish of different kind
Homeless lost or broken is what you will find
Go out and find someone be that fisher of men
Let them know they can be loved again

# A New Life

If I look to the world
I will get lost
If I continue this way
My life is the cost

There is this mystery
An unsolved story
We hear of this man
Who is the glory

He walked on some water
While healed the sick
Some people had claimed
What he did was a trick

People have tried
And could not succeed
To prove him a fake
And he's not what we need

But I will tell you this
He is more than just real
The healing is more
Than a drink or a pill

Don't be afraid
He is filled with a love
A peace and understanding
That fits better than a glove

Just lift up your hands
And open your heart
A new day begins
A new life to start

# A Purpose

The water rushes by
At a swift and flowing pace
The rapids on the rocks
Oh how I love this place

But as I sit and watch
A fish catches my eye
Fighting against the current
As others swim on by

He struggles and grows weak
Losing energy in this fight
The water pushes him
Until he is out of site

I wonder about that fish
The life he had is lost
Was he too afraid
His life was more the cost

And then I realized
That I am like that fish
No purpose in this life
Just living on a wish

Reliving in the moments
The moments when I failed
Living for myself
Myself I only hailed

So starting with today
A new life I will start
Living with a purpose
A purpose in my heart

# A Seed

The soil is ready
Moistened with rain
The seed to be sewn
The harvest to gain

The more that you have
The more you should give
To tithe to the Lord
Is the way you should live

Believe that he sees
When you give from your heart
Give til it hurts
Is where you should start

Our God will provide
Take care of your needs
Have faith in his word
Every word that he heeds

Give to Caesar that is his
Is what Jesus had taught
Give to God that belongs
Of your money or your lot

Put your God to the test
And you'll see what he'll do
He is a God of his word
Because he loves you

# A Warrior

As I wake in the morning
To another thankful day
I lift up my eyes
And hear what you say

Girt your loins with the truth
And the breastplate of
righteousness
Do not have fear
Be strong in your faithfulness

Taking the shield of faith
And the helmet of salvation
Anointed by the Lord
And praying with supplication

Take the sword of the spirit
Which is the word of God
Preparing the gospel of peace
Your feet will be shod

Pray with your heart
Be strong in your mind
Truth will be revealed
And peace you will find

It is time for your rest
Your fight is now done
Find yourself now
In the arms of the son

You have crossed over the river
From the earth you have gone
Here in this heaven
Your spirit lives on

A warrior you stood
You were never alone
Good and faithful servant
I welcome you home

# After The Class

The morning will come after the night
Rest will arrive after the fight
Good will be visible when the bad is done
Peace will prevail when the war has been won

We are able to hear when the yelling is no more
Soften your heart like never before
Be humble and gentle with love for one another
Be a model of patience to your sister and brother

Be quick to listen and slow to speak
Be the strength in God for the weary and weak
God gave is ears so we could hear
Quiet your mouth and wisdom you will hear

Anger will cause your mouth to run
Say some things that can't be undone
The enemy comes to kill steal and destroy
But deep in the Lord you will find the joy

Jesus is our teacher the one who will guide
He is the truth that no person can hide
The power in action we need in our walk
The word that we speak the love that we talk

When class is in session the student will learn
They will listen to the teacher knowledge they will earn
When the teacher is finished the class will be done
Wisdom will be gained and love will have won

# All In

This old dusty road with no end in site
The darkness consumes filled with fear and fright
The sounds that you hear as you walk down this trail
But deep in your heart you know you cannot fail

As you walk further in sounds start to stir
Sweat upon your brow you just aren't sure
But a whisper in your ear a breeze upon your face
You feel the Lord is near and filled with his grace

You step with great strength walk with confidence
Your work has just begun to bring the evidence
To spread the word of God to every corner of earth
The truth of our Lord that started with his birth

Visiting every country every mile of every land
Touching every heart helping the handicapped to stand
Acting as we should preaching every word
Until the nation's people are saved because they heard

Walk into the towns every house and every room
Sweeping every heart like the work of a broom
Believers that are force to go underground
Bring them to the light where the son can be found

You can't give a little or just a little fraction
God has called your name called you into action
He wants to see you full and filled from within
I ask you this question today are you All In

# All Together

Evening came and turned into night
Families together with love so bright
Preparing for bed with a final kiss
No one knew it would turn out like this

Police and fire patrolling their beat
Doctors and nurses exhausted on their feet
Pilots and passengers getting ready for flight
Too excited to sleep before next day's light

The next day arrives people out in the city
Going to work and acting so free
Employees coming to work bring the buildings alive
Like the honey bees collecting everything for the hive

But in a split second time had stood still
As the freedom we love was taken at will
A plane collides with a beautiful tower
Why can't we move where is our power

Stunned and silent it happened again
What is going on when will it end
When it was all over thousands had died
Many were grieving and millions had cried

But we all came together and we made a stand
We loved one another and gave all a hand
20 years have passed and this I can grant
We are all Ameri-can not Ameri-can't

# Always Near

What will I do
On the next day I wake
What can I do
To stand and not break

Where can I turn
When I'm broken and lost
How can I go on
When my life is the cost

I will look to the Lord
For this day that I have
I can stand on his word
To guide me down this path

The strength he supplies
I will take into war
He died on the cross
To give me much more

He is the Christ
Redeemer of all
When he calls his soldiers
I will answer the call

A sheppard to his flock
He knows us by name
The fire in our hearts
The great and mighty flame

Do not worry
And do not fear
Be silent in this moment
He is always near

# ANCHOR

The sea is rough and the waves are strong
Being tossed around holding on too long
I pray everyday waiting to here from you
I don't know which way to turn or what to do

The world is noisy and it's hard to here
The evil and his lies spreading all the fear
Where is my path where is the road
I'm lost in a fog carrying this load

But then I realized what I have done
The battles I fought that could have been won
I've been listening to the world and not God's word
The things I've been told the things that I've heard

But now is the time this boat come to a stop
No longer on the bottom I'm going to the top
When I am weak the Lord makes me strong
With him as my rock i just can't go wrong

I'm dropping my anchor and lowering my sail
Maintaining my faith with him I can't fail
Let go of the noise and seek for the peace
Drop your anchor in him he is your increase

# Angel Among Us

Every once in awhile someone comes along
Who steps up and says I will be the one
Who gives of themselves to teach the little children
And show them learnings fun

The patience of a saint to do it everyday
To teach a little boy learning with autism
And teach them they are light
Like the beautiful reflection of a prism

We thank you for your service
Even though we realize
You are more valuable
You are an angel in our eyes

From the time that they arrive
To the time they take the bus
You are more than just a teacher
You are an angel among us

# Antenna

A static sound
Is all that you hear
The music or voices
All are unclear

You reach for the dial
To change to a station
For something to listen
A latest compilation

It doesn't really help
Til you adjust one more thing
The antenna is the tool
For the words it will bring

We are the antenna
Between God and this world
We connect to his voice
Every boy and every girl

The connection is strong
And never be lost
His grace as his mercy
Will cover the cost

So just as the antenna
Brings the world the latest news
Be his antenna
With the words we should choose

Take the words that he says
And the message he gives
To spread to the hearts
And the life that he lives

Connect to the station
That is always real strong
The station of his heart
The most beautiful song

# BACA

It is the rolling thunder
That you can hear for miles
The sound of a roar
That brings a thousand smiles

They do not have wings
Or halos over head
Just a friendship that is wanted
And a confidence instead

They stand up for the people
The victims of abuse
To show them of their worth
Love is what they use

They come from different backgrounds
Different genders different races
Together for the same cause
With love from different places

None of them are paid
They volunteer their time
They pay for all the costs
Every dollar every dime

The greatest thing they give
Is love to everyone
A confidence to win
A comfort when they are done

The next time that you see
These angels riding through
Make a path for them
BACA and their crew

# Believe

You deal with their taunting
And teasing too
Your overgrown teeth
And flat hairdo

You deal with their hate
As they call you a name
Your parents are not rich
Or have loads of fame

With every day
It does not seem to end
You long to belong
You wish for a friend

You are not alone
Others feel the same pain
But believe in yourself
There is more left to gain

Inside of your body
Inside of your heart
Is a strength that you have
You've had from the start

You are greater than them
You can concur anything
To overcome mountains
And comfort to bring

Believe in yourself
Stand tall and proud
Let your voice be heard
It is mighty and loud

# Bend a knee for the Lord

I remember the day before class would start
We would stand by our desk with our hand on our heart
We didn't care if it was good or bad
We stood and pledged to the American flag

But in this day they say it's discrimination
To have pride and love this wonderful nation
Athletes and celebrities are taking a knee
Showing that they have no loyalty

Turning their backs on those
who serve
They cry and whine and have the nerve
To say the police are killing the blacks
They riot and loot the stores in attacks

They have taken God out of the gov't and school
If you don't believe as them you are called a fool
They claim it's a right to kill a fetus
They delete your posts if you mention Jesus

We need to take a stand and come together
We will fight the fight no matter the weather
Protect our rights to bear arms and speech
We will regain this country and further the reach

The reach of the people and the patriots everywhere
From coast to coast this view we share
Return our country to the way before
Stand for the flag and bend a knee for the Lord

# Bold Faith

Some feel empty, While others feel full
Some try to push it away, While others continue to pull

Believers have it, Though they cannot see
You can fill up your life, What can this be

It is faith that we have, A belief in the word
A belief in a savior, Based on just what we've heard

A faith that can move, Mountains into the sea
A faith without fear, A faith greater than me

Fight with a faith, That lifts you off the floor
It gives you the strength, And throws open the door

Faith looks forward, It does not look back
It keeps you on your path, Faith keeps you on track

A faith that is powerful, A faith that is bold
A faith more valuable, Than silver and gold

So fill with this faith, Fill yourself til your full
Bold faith in our God, The Lord eternal

# Bow Our Heads

Wherever they serve
On air land or sea
Fighting for our rights
Our right to be free

Go in as a child
Come out so much more
Serving in peace
Some serving in war

A man or a woman
Weathered by time
But inside their heart
A warrior you will find

A blank check they gave
At the time that they signed
Made out to the country
Their one of a kind

Some lost a limb
Maybe even all four
Some lost more than that
In the hell of a tour

Returned in a box
Covered by a flag
A memory to others
And the life that they had

So, we take off our hats
And then bow our head
To the sacrifice given
No words can be said

# Break The Chains

The chains are broken
Released from my soul
My heart is new
Freedom Is my goal

No longer a slave
Held captive by fear
My saviour saved me
He holds me near

Thrown in the fire
I cried out to him
The flames did not touch
My faith from within

Condemned by the world
In his Holy name
Like the hatred he felt
We will feel the same

If we stand with the world
We will be judged by the Lord
But if we stand with the Lord
We will be judged by his word

For God did not send
His son to condemn
But to save of this world
From the evil filled within

So break all the chains
That are holding you back
Take hold of your life
No longer under attack

# Bring The Rain

The feeling of spring
The smell of fresh rain
New life begins
New adventures to gain

New crops planted
The seed to sprout
The harvest will be great
Great without a doubt

But while we wait
What should we do
Should we drop down to our knees
Or cry out from a pew

We can do both
Or stand out in a field
For Jesus is our rock
Our salvation and shield

I pray unto you Lord
For your mercy and your grace
I cry out for your favor
I seek your Holy face

I have sewn the seed
I seek your Holy shower
Your blessings to come down
Show us your glory and power

We will pray and wait
For the harvest and the gain
Soak us in the light
We ask you bring the rain

# Build A Bridge

Is there someone in your life
That is lost and alone
Searching for a purpose
Searching for a home

You know you want to help
But don't know what to do
It feels like a valley
Stands between them and you

Just open up your heart
With faith of a mustard seed
Share the love of God
God will provide your need

Your need to spread the love
The emptiness you can fill
Just teach the Holy word
You can do God's will

You should also understand
No two people are the same
We come from different nations
Different beliefs of how we came

We must extend to all we can
An ear to hear their story
A hand that reaches out
Yet gives our God the glory

So start to build a bridge
Connect to every soul
That then they are made new
In Christ you are made whole

# Build Us Up

One step forward and two steps back
It takes all I have to keep me on track
This world that we live is falling apart
The churches and cities are losing their heart

The enemy has built division with a wall
We pray in your name that it soon will fall
Send your army of angels to protect all our young
Supply all the tools until the war has been won

Grow us in spirit so we can be like you
Build up our faith, strength and trust too
Put people in our life like our heavenly father
Someone to watch and be our daily spotter

Guide my path through the old and the wise
Let me gain wisdom greater than the enemy's lies
Bring us together in your heavenly light
Be our commander as we go through this fight

Where two or more are gathered there you are
Give us a heart for community and we will go far
What would you do in times of the worst
Jesus we know you would love first

# Call On His Name

The clouds that hang
Above the ground below
Some with rain
And some with snow

A brisk fall wind
Blows the east to the west
A chill in the air
With the end of harvest

Those who have sewn
Now reap the reward
With the faith in our Lord
And a heart to look forward

A time will come
When the sun will shine
A new day arrives
A new day reminds

Reminds of the future
A future that is bright
When we follow the Lord
The Lord is our light

The light in our darkness
The path for our feet
A comfort to the broken
Strength when we feel weak

No matter what happens
Or what may appear
Just call on his name
And let go of the fear

# Cast Your Sin

There will come a time
There will come a place
When we all stand before
The Lord's holy face

We will be judged
For everything we've done
Account for every moment
Everything from day one

If you have ever stole
Or told a white lie
Our past will come before
When we meet him in the sky

But let me tell you something
A secret you should know
Something you should do
Before it's time to go

Just drop down to your knees
And repent of all your sin
Ask him for forgiveness
And he will let you in

Don't worry about tomorrow
Forget about your past
Just live in today
Your problems he has cast

No longer knows your sin
Your faith in him is best
He has cast your sin
As far as the east is from the west

# Clear The Way

Famine and drought with talk of wars
Locked down at home churches close doors
Lovers of self-haters of others
Filled with a hate and killers of brothers

Good will be evil and evil will be good
Burning of all even crosses made of wood
Liars and looters riots and disease
A person will come and all will appease

Claims he will bring to all world peace
But hell will reveal and hell will release
A pain never seen and pain never felt
Is greater than the body has even been dealt

But there is one who is greater than all
One who will lift everyone when they fall
Riding on the clouds trumpets heard loud
Light so bright that covers the crowd

Make way for the king the bringer of light
The one strong enough to win this spiritual fight
Clear the way clear the street
Everybody on their knees no one on their feet

Angels will be heard singing glory and praise
The time has come for the end of days
He will win this war the battles no more
Call on his name before the end game

# Come As The Children

Let the little children come
By car or plane or boat
Coming by the millions
To the Lord's Holy throne

Teaching them with love
And building with the strength
Showing them with Jesus
There is no greater gain

Some cultures teach their young
To hate others and to kill
They do not know the Lord
Or live by or father's will

Our children are the future
To walk by foot this land
To reach the list and sick
And be the helping hand

Listen to the words
That Jesus stood and spoke
To every heart that heard
And the dead that he awoke

You will feel the spirit
Come rushing like a wind
And flooding across the land
Every door it will go in

The lives that will be changed
By those who go before
Will feel the healing power
By Jesus who is Lord

The peace will overwhelm
The power will be great
The love is everlasting
The grace will fill your plate

# Come Together

People walking around through the wind and the storm
With a fear of change and stepping out of the norm
Connected by a computer with a single strand of wire
Trying to get the views and likes numbers higher

Separated by belief and divided by our race
The only thing to save us is his mercy and his grace
We must come together stop fighting with each other
Start treating everyone like our sister or our brother

Evil comes to kill steal and destroy
We must curb all the hate and replace it with joy
Spread love on this land and peace in the air
No matter our skin or color of our hair

We must come together and join hand in hand
Together we fall and together we stand
Rise up in this day and your voice will be heard
Like the chorus of angels or songs from a bird

On the wings of an eagle flying high above a cloud
Evil must leave when his name is screamed out loud
The name of our Lord our savior from above
We can all come together in his name and his love

# Courageous

No matter how big
No matter how small
No matter how short
No matter how tall

We all have a reason
In this world is a place
Where we can feel safe
And filled with his grace

But there comes a time
A time to step out
To live in our faith
Our voice with a shout

The strength that we need
Comes from courage that we have
Like the seas that were parted
By Moses with a staff

Or David with a rock
In a fight with no sword
Filled with a love
And strong faith in the Lord

We all need to step
From our own comfort zone
Light the flame of your faith
You are not alone

The reward will be greater
Then the risk that can be
Be courageous in him
Sharing love faithfully

# Creator

He has no borders
You can't put him in a box
He will not be contained
By steel chains or locks

He cannot be contained
Within a box or a line
He is greater than the world
And larger than all time

Why do some people
Try and hold him down
Put limits on him
And steal back the crown

He is the great author
And creator of all
The author of salvation
Creator to even the small

He carries all the wisdom
Every life is in his hand
He strengthens all the weak
On ocean and on land

No one can overcome
And steal his Holy fire
He reigns from heaven above
He does not rest or tire

Just call out to his name
He's seated on the throne
His grace is everlasting
His love is always shown

# Darkest Before The Light

The sun doesn't rise
Until later in the morn
The days keep getting colder
Until new life is reborn

Things start to break
Situations will go wrong
Winter will have the feeling
Of being extremely long

People will feel tired
When the sun is gone for days
Longing for the time
To see its beautiful rays

Depression may set in
Loneliness will too
With no place we can go
Everything frozen in our view

But do not let the sadness
Be like darkness in the night
Be patient with the world
And soon you'll see the light

For everything there is a time
A time that it will take
A moment of a rest
Then beauty it will make

Just seek the Lord for strength
And guidance through this fight
And remember that each day
Is darkest before the light

# Dear God

Dear God it's me
I love you so
How to pray
I do not know

Do I say thank you
For things you have done
Should I rejoice
For the battles are won

What do I say
Or what do I do
How do I know
My prayers are heard too

I'm just a small child
The least of all these
Like a falling spring rain
Or a gentle small breeze

Please tell me God
Just what should I say
How should I act
Or what should I pray

I'll wait for your answer
However it may come
In the form of a sound
Or a light from the sun

Mommy and Daddy
They don't have the time
To teach me to pray
Or what I should find

Please guide my soul
And help me find love
The kind that you get
Only from above

I hope you heard this
I make it my choice
To listen for you God
In your heavenly voice

# Do Not Fear

365 times
We are told not to fear
Do not worry or stress
If the Lord's voice you hear

He says He is the life
The truth and the way
With him you'll never thirst
You will be filled every day

We are consumed by a shadow
He guides us with his light
He overtakes the dark
His love for us shines bright

No longer will we fear
Afraid to walk this road
We were not meant to carry
The burden of this load

Your struggles will be no more
Lay your problems at the throne
Grow your faith in the Lord
Your path will be shown

Don't become discouraged
When you are facing a new test
Just keep your faith in him
And know that you are blessed

Blessed are those who thirst
And seek the righteousness
For they will be filled
With our father's peacefulness

# Everywhere

We serve a God
Who loves unconditional
No matter who we are
Different or traditional

He loves all the people
No matter where they are
He loves everyone
From the near to the far

You can find him in a jail
On a seat in a bar
In a hospital room
While you're crying in a car

He's not on a mountain
Or sitting in a throne
He is right there beside you
Even in your home

Some people believe
That he is nowhere
That he is not here
Nor is he even there

But our God is mighty
He is mighty to care
He wants you to have faith
That he is everywhere

# Extend A Hand

The paths we follow
Here in this life
May cross with some
Our husband or wife

But we cannot forget
Those who stand
Next to our path
Or in other land

We need to remember
To reach out to those
Who lack of the word
The water and clothes

No matter their color
Their race or their creed
We are all created
With a life and a need

A need to be close
A need to hear
Of the God that loves us
The God that is near

So we must build a bridge
To reach all the lost
To show them the love
The life that it cost

Jesus paid the price
Because of the love
He extended a hand
With a love from above

# Faith

When a sailor fights the waves to reach the beach
Or a hiker climbing looks for the next rock to reach
Our Lord is at work and will calm the seas
Miracles still happen in the healing of disease

He sits on the throne still to this day
Clearing the path of those who lost their way
When we are falling we need to look up
When we are thirsty he gives us a cup

Jesus loves me this I know
For the bible tells me so
We have learned from an early time
I am his and he is mine

We drop to our knees and pray each night
We lay our problems down for him to fight
He says rest my child let me take this one
I will show you now how this war is won

I will wrap my loving arms around
Hold you tight until the cure is found
I am your savior I am your Lord
I have held your hand ever since you were born

Put your faith in me and trust in my heart
Before you know it you will have a new start
Things won't be easy but remember my love
Of the father who created everything from above

# Fishers of Man

The boat sits alone out on the lake
The waters still without a wake
Patiently waiting for the catch to appear
Faithfully listening for your voice to hear

But that single boat doesn't have the strength
To pull in the blessing or go to the length
Where two or more are so will I be
Is the instruction Christ gave for those who believe

Planted in the Lord is where we must stand
To win all the souls every woman and man
Two churches working doing God's will
Two boats together have more space to fill

Commit to the Lord commit to one another
Take to the streets every sister every brother
Follow the guidance the Lord has to give
He will supply our needs for to live

We are not enemies we are teammates with a mission
We must come together to achieve the Lord's vision
One net alone will not be enough
To bring in the catch as the waters get rough

But two nets combined two churches together
Will bring a greater catch no matter the weather
Hand in hand heart with heart
We are fishers of men and will do our part

# Follow My Voice

The sounds are flooding inside my head
Telling me to follow them instead
Whispers and voices telling what I should do
They drown out the voice the voice of you

The voices you hear will lead to destruction
But the voice of our God will lead with instruction
We cannot see him but we know he is there
He will not leave you or lead you to despair

The enemy will lie because he wants to destroy
Your place in this world and all of your joy
Just silence the noise that he tries to make
Use the power within and your life you'll retake

Have faith in the voice the one that is true
Trust in his way as he walks you through
He will help you climb the mountains before
Will help you cross the oceans to shore

Pray to the one who is creator of all
Believe when I tell you he will answer the call
He calmly says just follow my voice
He will see you through so you can rejoice

# Forgive

How can someone
In all the sorrow and pain
Let go of the past
As the ashes remain

The ashes from a fire
With a flame out of control
That tears your inside up
And wears at all your soul

Words that don't build up
But continue to break down
The dreams that you once had
Come crashing all around

How can a person change
Into a brand new man
No longer full of anger
On Holy values stand

The answer to the question
Is inside an old book
The bible is filled with pages
Like a recipe for a cook

Just follow the directions
And soon then you will see
You've let go of the pain
And filled with great mercy

Forgive is God's command
Forgive and it's made new
The past is now forgotten
Just like he has promised you

# From The Start

When we are born our time began
The time to grow into the best we can
We are taught to love and learn to trust
Our mom and dad and those closest to us

We don't know the number of days to live
Or the amount of love we are able to give
We will lose some of those close to our heart
But until that time comes we will do our part

Our part in this world and this place that we know
Through all the pain we will continue to grow
I just wish I could make a phone call to you
A call up to heaven that God would let through

And then one day God whispered in my ear
Just speak from your heart and your prayer I will hear
Can you pass on our message to the ones that we love
They are here with me in my kingdom above

They are not in pain they are whole once again
No sadness in their heart just love within
You know we will grieve and wonder why
Our loved one is gone so early in time

You will give us the strength and comfort our heart
Like you have in the past like you have from the start
Will you give them a hug for me one more time
As we wait on this earth in our place in the line

# Full Time Faith

I will believe
Even though I cannot see
I will trust
The love you have for me

I will build my faith
To use in every day
Not just when I think I need it
I will have a full-time faith

Not faith for just a season
Spring, summer, winter, fall
Or when I am in trouble
My faith will be my call

I'll share my faith each day
To share with many others
Show how to strengthen faith
With sisters and our brothers

Just like the stars above
Let my faith shine bright
A faith that's seen from miles
Like a galaxy in the night

My faith will not be faint
Nor will it be weak
My faith will be made strong
To spread among the meek

This full-time faith I have
Is grounded in his word
A faith that fills this life
The greatest ever heard

# Get Up And Stand

The water is rising, with waves all around
I'm being overtaken, and no lifeboat to be found
I look for a ladder, or even a rope
I'm being pulled further, and losing all hope

The addiction I have, is the weight like a stone
The path I have taken, has left me alone
I'm filled with an anger, and living in sin
I have no feeling, of value within

The screaming and lies, is all that is heard
But with still small voice, he is sharing his word
Laying on the floor, I see an image of a hand
And a voice telling me, to get up and stand

My past is behind, and my future is ahead
I am alive in the Lord, and no longer dead
Created by a father, in his image from above
He asks for our faith, and obedience in love

Like a plant that will grow when you put it in light
Get out of the dark, and he will win the fight
The enemy lies in our face, and continues deceit
He puts you in sin, and knocks you off your feet

This battle will grow and consume all your heart
But if you turn to the Lord and make a new start
He will guide all your steps down the narrow way
He is our salvation through obedience today

Where are those that accuse you of sin
Neither do I, let your new life begin
Turn away from old ways, you are made new
And fill with this love, I will always have for you

# GIFTS

He's sitting by the lake
Feeling the breeze against his face
The birds continue singing
Never a better place

Skipping rocks out on the lake
Watching the little pebbles roll
The circles that they make
Is medicine for the soul

Walking through the woods
The leaves under your feet
The rustling of the branches
From the calm and gentle breeze

Underneath the stars
On a clear and peaceful night
Or the colors that are made
From the sun's rising light

The rain that gently falls
Or the crickets that you hear
The animals that come out
And the deer that soon appear

These are just a few
Of the blessings that we have
In this world that we live
A gift from God's own hand

The next time you are out
Or if you're sitting by a tree
Be thankful for the gifts
That God has given thee

# God of the Outcome

The tears flow like the river Nile
The blood is splashed for a greater mile
The pain we feel consumes each day
What can we do to go a better way

We don't feel connected the signal is dead
Why do we feel this pressure in our head
What should we do which way should we turn
Peace in our lives the lessons to learn

We look for the answers to this rigorous test
The Lord is the answer who will give us the rest
It is not our place to know God's plan
Everything is possible because the Lord can

The tears that have fallen will stay in the ground
God will grow trees and plants all around
The blood that is shed will continue to flow
God will build nations with love he will show

When we start a marathon we cannot see the end
We don't know what sits around every bend
We should trust in the Lord in every word
Continue the faith until the trumpets are heard

He is waiting for us every step of the way
Patient in our lives from the beginning of every day
Lift up your hands high into the air
He listens to your word your thoughts and your prayer

Stand in obedience and trust in this war
He will deliver to us greater than before
He is faithful to all every corner you are from
He promises that he is the God of outcome

# God Who Hears Me

I walk in my days
Through all this evil land
With my eyes looking forward
And my Bible in hand

My past is behind
My future before
It seems where I go
Is another closed door

I pray from the heart
And listen with my ear
Cry so many tears
But from him I not hear

Is me it that did wrong
Is it me, am I bad
I seek out your voice
Please speak to me dad

With a thundering sound
It soon became clear
He has not left me
Close, he stands near

I can hear you now
My future, I can see
My life in your hands
God, who hears me

# God With Us

He came as a child, who was born in a manger
Born for all men, women and stranger
He grew into a man, unlike the others
He healed the sick, with his sisters and brothers

He guides the path through every storm
He covers the outcast and keeps them warm
He gives hope to the hopeless
And shelter to the homeless

Like the instrument panel, for the pilot of a plane
Or the railroad tracks for the conductor of a train
He will part the waters and calm all the seas
He is the king of kings and the prince of peace

Gave sight to the blind and strength to the weak
He taught to forgive, gave confidence to meek
He will walk by our side and not leave us alone
He will rule with love, as he reigns from the throne

Put your trust in him and faith in his name
Even if you are beaten and forced into shame
He knows every path and will make it straight
He will bring you home through the narrow gate

He humbles us all everyday that we live
Love for our neighbour, and teaches us to give
He raises us up from the grave like Lazarus
His name is Emmanuel, God with us

## God's Message Through Music

We are the little children,
Of our Father God
The one who made this world,
The water, trees, and sod.

We come here from your kingdom,
And known you from before
We will always want to seek you,
And want to know you more.

We live to always serve you,
Not into the enemy's potions
But continue to follow your will,
And not just through the motions.

Our strength arises high,
As we wait upon the Lord
We're always growing stronger,
As we walk in the Holy Word.

We follow what you told us,
To forgive seventy times seven
Not to boost our own ego
But to see the smiles from Heaven.

You've told me a million times,
And to open my eyes and see
That because He loves us all,
To stand and say, "I Am Free".

The time will soon come,
When you lift the Holy sheet
Your love is what we seek,
Please Word of God speak.

The sun will always rise,
With the coming of everyday
Even if I fall or sin,
I know that you love me anyway.

The power of the love,
The times I want to cry
The blessings you give me,
I still ask "Who Am I"

There will be a day,
Of no more pain or fears
Just plenty of love and hugs,
And Angels bringing good cheers.

The Lord is soon coming,
To the earth He'll find His way
To take us home with Him,
On that blessed Glorious Day.

So when you need some music,
The music from above
Keep turning the radio dial,
Until you find Love.

Each night you look at the stars, you are not only seeing God, but you are seeing the notes to the most beautiful song yet to be heard. When that song is revealed, we will know the Lord's coming is near.

# Greater Is The Love

I have on my armor
My breast plate is on too
The helmet of salvation
All to fight for you

But the greatest weapon we have
Comes in a different form
A book that's filled with love
The story of how it's born

Good is stronger than bad
Love is stronger than hate
Evil has no place
In this world that he gave

We must stand together
Greater is the love
We have for one another
We receive from God above

Go to the corners of the earth
Every nation, tribe and tongue
Spread our Father's word
The battle will be won

From sea to every sea
The dessert and the plains
The mountains in the sky
Through wind and driving rains

We will not be stopped
The work that we will do
Will defeat the evil
Through him that is the truth

# Guiding Light

With the past in the mirror
As the future stands before
A new year has come
With opportunities galore

A new day arrives
To live like day one
With goals in our sight
And times to have fun

Resolutions are set
The dreams that we have
The memories we make
The past that we had

Everything has been built
The path has been made
With one step ahead
Our start will be great

We take the first
Down the dusty old road
The weight on our shoulders
Trying to carry the load

How can we carry
Everything by our self
It just can't be done
Without some other help

Then he appears
To carry the weight
To give us a rest
Give our shoulders a break

He takes on the world
Because he loves us
This is a man
I know I can trust

He only asks me
To show neighbors some love
And live in this world
Like a hand fits a glove

Who is this man
Who will take on the fight
He is the way, the truth, the life
He is Christ, the guiding light

# He Came

He came as a king
But he came to serve
He came for the least
Yet he did not want served

He healed of the sick
Taught people how to sow
He spoke of the word
Taught people how to grow

You take what you have
In the poor you invest
Believe in your actions
And reap a harvest

Go out in our towns
Spread out in the land
Every person you reach
Is a piece in the band

The band of believers
A band of the strong
We all work together
Every voice in this song

Use your voice at this time
Don't stop until you're heard
Pray in all moments
Together we'll learn

The spirit will flow
And fill all the hearts
Bring you closer to God
Your discipleship starts

# HE IS

When two people decide
To come together as one
They have made a choice
That should not come undone

They enter a marriage
A display of their love
A bond that will hold
When push comes to shove

But others have found
When they do it alone
The marriage stalls out
When it should have grown

Then they see what is missing
What's missing is the glue
He created the world
Every color and hue

He is God the father
He is waiting for you
To invite him to be a part
And a blessing of new

A new life as a couple
A forever so great
He is always on time
And his time is never late

Enjoy your new life
As you exchange each a ring
Your forever starts now
Filled with grace from the king

# HEROES

As the lights go out
On another day
The workday is done
We go our separate way

Return to a home
The kids and the wife
A home that we have
A better way of life

But just when you thought
The town would go to sleep
The chaos arises
The police try to keep

They give of themselves
To protect the small town
They go without lunch
Chasing criminals down

The doctors and nurses
Working hard through the night
The fire-fighters work
Against a fire they fight

Paramedics work to save
Every person that they see
These are the heroes
Who jump instantly

They all are not perfect
Nowhere even close
They just serve with a heart
In a profession that they chose

# His Blood

The world has seen many who like to stir the pot
Some who fill with anger that they have been taught
Brothers against brothers sisters against mothers
People who scream and shout in the faces of all others

Good has become bad and bad are truth and facts
The normal has become riots and violent acts
Cancel every culture and history the world believes
To change the world today with the evil it achieves

Followers of Christ need stand and spread the light
People of peace arise to help in this spiritual fight
No person in this world is better than another
Our value in God's eyes is the same for every brother

How do we interact with people of a different view
We try to spread the truth of God to just a few
Just like a drop of rain can turn into a flood
The word of God can spread and shower with the blood

The fight we fight today is a fight for the soul
The world is filled with evil trying to consume the whole
Take your helmet and your shield your breastplate and your sword
We fight this Holy battle we fight it for the Lord

The enemy has come and his time is running out
He is attacking every person he has come with a shout
He attacks God's kingdom looking for the weak
But the Lord will make them strong even in the meek

# His DNA

The God of this world
Made me with his DNA
You look in my blood
And see a cross display

Filled with his love
His grace and mercy
Made in his image
Is what you do see

A child of royalty
The DNA of a king
More valuable than gold
Or a diamond in a ring

Through faith in the Lord
We are children in a union
We take of the bread
And wine in communion

Let him take you in his arms
With a seat on his lap
And listen to him teach
Of the way and the path

For those who are lead
By the spirit of the Lord
Will share in his glory
When you follow his word

Now if we are the children
Then we are the heir
With Christ in the kingdom
Together we will share

# His Mercy

Why would a god
Who is loving and good
Allow this evil
I wish I understood

Dying in the streets
And fighting over land
Diseases are spreading
It has gotten out of hand

This fallen world
Filled with the sin
Evil in the hearts
Corrupt from within

Which way can we go
The direction to turn
Before we are lost
In hell left to burn

His name is the Christ
The one that we seek
He is filled with the love
And the truth he does speak

It is not our God
Who turned the world dark
But the sins of the people
That chose of this mark

The only way out
Of this darkness we see
Is turn to the Lord
And feel his mercy

# His Voice

I am broken
I am a sinner
I am lost
I don't feel like a winner

These tears that I cry
Come from the deep
I don't have the strength
This mountain is too steep

I feel defeated
I have lost this war
I cannot go online
Cannot fight anymore

And out of the silence
A still small voice
Telling me to rest
Having faith is my choice

He says he never left
Standing always by my side
Even when I ran
And attempted to hide

Every tear that I wept
He holds in his hand
He picks me up now
Tells me to stand

Inside my heart
Is where it will begin
With the roar of a lion
He says the battle he will win

Death is defeated
My sins are all gone
He is the Rock
My life is built on

So when I feel lost
I will listen for his voice
And know I have reason
In him I will rejoice

# Hope

The enemy is swift
The enemy is invisible
But if we all work together
Anything is possible

It comes to steal
Kill and destroy
But in God's mercy
Peace we will enjoy

It circles the world
Leaving death in its path
But if we work as one
We will overcome the aftermath

Hope is what we need
Hope is a prayer
Give us the strength
To heal our people everywhere

Healing to the sick
Strength to the weak
To the leaders in this world
Down to the poor and meek

We pray for comfort
The wisdom we need
To care for the broken
Every mouth that we feed

When the end is near
When we see the light
We will win this war
As your grace shines bright

# I Can I Will

Created in his image
In him I say I can
I will become the best
Created by I am

The people of this world
No matter where they are
Are children of this God
His children near and far

He created Adam and Eve
And others at the start
To love and be together
And never be apart

He created the whole world
And everything that flies above
The fish inside the seas
He did it out of love

Everything we need
Was provided at the start
The power to move mountains
With the faith from within our heart

I can do all things
Through Christ who strengthens me
In him I find the power
His grace and his mercy

I will tell myself
I can I will I am
With positive in my life
Next to him I stand

# I Can

I can believe
In what I can become
I can believe
Even where I have come from

I believe what I can do
What I set upon my heart
I believe what I can do
When I take the steps to start

I believe what I can be
When I find the strength inside
I believe what I can be
When I quit trying to hide

I will become a person
That stands out in a crowd
I will become a person
Whose voice is loud and proud

I am going to be
The person my family needs
I am going to be
The hero my children sees

Today is the beginning
The first day in this life
My past no longer matters
The future is my light

# In The Arms

A simple smile
When we'd see your face
A firm handshake
When we'd visit your place

Coco would run
To see who was there
Her tail would be going
As she run everywhere

You shown a kindness
Like no other I knew
A heart for the Lord
And a soul that was true

Your work here is done
You have earned your reward
A place in the kingdom
In the arms of the Lord

Tears will be shed
And we will be sad
When we think of the times
And the memories we had

But we will rejoice
As we seek out his light
Just knowing you're home
And you finished the fight

We know that we
Will see you again
In the arms of the Lord
In the heavens within

# In The Presence

From the mountains of Colorado
To the sunsets of Hawaii
His love spreads far and wide
Over the land and the sea

And his love fills
The believers heart
And a faith that knows
You will never be apart

It takes a special kind of person
Who wakes with the attitude
Thankful for each day
And expresses their gratitude

A smile that shines
And a light in their eye
Feeling so blessed
Our Lord is nearby

But there comes a time
Thanks to his sacrifice
When we are called home
To be with him in paradise

Those left behind
Filled with sorrow and grief
Will trust in the Lord
Holding onto their belief

That this is not goodbye
Your work here is done
They will see you once again
In the presence of the son

# In This Together

Two babies born
On the same day
In the same hospital
In the month of May

Both were born with hearts
Their blood the color red
One with curly black hair
The other with a bald head

They came into this world
Innocence all within
The only difference they have
Is the color of their skin

They were born into this world
Filled with love and not hate
They will play and grow together
Inseparable to this date

They don't see the difference
They only see a friend
They enjoy the other so
And laugh until the end

Just like these two
We are born with a love
And when we leave this earth
We return to the father above

We are all a gift
Let's stand in life as one
We are all in this together
And spread love to everyone

# In Your Presence

With happiness and joy we enter this earth
The best is the moment during a child's birth
We learn to roll over and we learn how to walk
Silence is now gone when we learn how to talk

We grow older learning new things day after day
Following the steps and learning the way
We do not worry about the days that remain
We need to push on through all of the pain

We don't know the number of days that we'll live
Or the time with our family and love we can give
We need to trust that our God has control
When he takes us home we will be made whole

As the heavens are higher and greater are his ways
We believe that his will can protect all our days
Don't be afraid for our lord we will meet
In the presence of our God while we walk the golden street

# Invite Him

Stuck in a rut
This weight upon me
I try to get out
Unable to break free

This life is going nowhere
The pressure on my back
I feel so lost and weak
As the enemy continues to attack

What options do I have
Which direction can I turn
I need strength to overcome
The wisdom I can learn

His name is Jesus Christ
He is the prince of peace
The mighty king of kings
In him you'll find release

Just drop down to your knees
Leave your problems at the throne
Find your faith inside
He will not leave you alone

He gave Samson all his strength
And Moses the confidence
He saved Noah and his family

He gave Israel independence
He knows your every need
He'll forgive your every sin
Put your trust in him
Invite him to live within

# Let Go

My head in my hands
No strength to go on
The days seem so dark
Just waiting for the dawn

The voices in my head
Never seem to stop
They fight for my soul
I need help to get to the top

My life was at peace
I used to be strong
What changed in my life
Where did I go wrong

We have all had this feeling
A fight in our head
Some found the direction
Others gave up instead

What can we do
Where can we go
Which way do we turn
We just do not know

The first step to take
Is find a listening ear
Find faith in your life
Let go of the fear

Then you will start
To grow and to heal
Open your heart
His love you will feel

# Let Him Be Your Lord

Planes over head cars on the street
We rush everywhere places to be
We wish that we had more time in our day
In a panic we push people out of our way

Our homes are a mess our lives are the same
The clock is ticking down like it does in a game
We are missing the joy in this life we are meant
Trying to make money for food and for rent

The one we are missing is standing at the door
He's ready to help like he has done before
Excuses we make say we don't have the time
We lie to ourselves when we say things are fine

Everyday he will come as you hear him knock
He wants to be more for you like a rock
The rock of salvation the drink when we thirst
Put everything aside so he can be first

The problems you have lay down at his throne
Believe in his love you are never alone
So the next time you hear that knock on your door
Just open it up let him be your Lord

# Life Change

Can you feel it, it might feel strange
A pounding in your heart, a pounding for life change
That is the Lord, consuming with a fire
A fire of change, you can only get from higher

Voices are heard, shouting out your praise
We worship you now and all the coming days
We will travel to the lands and walk down every street
Witness to the poor and every person that we meet

Can you feel it now, the love and the grace
The peace and mercy flooding every place
The winds of change like a wave that blows
It will not end until every person knows

He has cleared the path and shown the road
He wants you to rest and give him your load
Let go of the past and look to the future
His love is genuine holy and pure

Are you ready for the change ready for a start
Ready for the power of faith coming from your heart
You can come to his house and won't be alone
You will see a great change when you come into his house

# Lift Me Up

Lift me up to the place you want for me
Lift me up to the highest I can be
Help me to stand on the mountain top
Where I will praise you and will not stop

The waters will rise above the shore
But you will protect me like you've done before
My faith is strong I believe in your glory
My life is but just an unfinished story

I will build my house upon this rock
You are the Shepard and we are your flock
I drop to my knees and raise my hands above
I seek your strength comfort and love

I will arm myself with a shield and sword
I am your soldier and you are my Lord
You will give me the wisdom i need
I will show love through the people I feed

I want people to see you living in me
Me shining a light for everyone to see
The flame that I am is greater than the dark
You are the author in me make your mark

# Little Steps

The little steps
Running down the hall
Your smiling face
When I rolled you a ball

The birthdays you had
And Christmases with cheer
The pleasure we had
To have you here

The time we have
Goes by too fast
But we'll always remember
The beautiful past

Just a little boy
Grown into a man
The passion you had
To follow God's plan

You were taken away
Much too soon
In the arms of the father
With a heavenly tune

We will not forget
The times that we had
With you in our lives
The good and the bad

Go rest in the kingdom
With the Lord up on high
We will see you again
This is not good bye

# Love One Another

Fear is strong
But faith is stronger
Hate's reach is long
But love's is longer

A lack of hope
Is what we see
A fear that controls
The whole country

People have lost
A sense of worth
How to love one another
We've learned since birth

Neighbor against neighbor
Brother against brother
Now more than ever
We need to love one another

Love for the older
And love for the young
No partisan politics
Come together as one

So if you see
Someone in need
Someone who's lost
Someone to feed

Spread with them hope
A meaning to live
A change for tomorrow
A more reason to give

# Love Until It Hurts

He came into the world just a baby boy
God made into man to show the world joy
He studied in the temples at such a young age
A teacher to the people the world was his stage

The high priest in the church accused him of blasphemy
But he still taught his flock and didn't abuse his authority
He loved the sick and sinners and even the tax collector
He searched out all the hurt and tried to make them better

He knew his time was short and one day it would come
But he still displayed love knowing his work was not done
Taken in the night he was betrayed by a kiss
His love for the world was greater than his wish

He wished his cup removed along with all the pain
But the world needed him if they every wanted gain
Gain entry to the kingdom and spend eternity
Forgiven of their sins he was their diety

Punished for the sins of all the mankind
He had a greater love no man would ever find
Beaten with a rod that removed pieces of skin
But nothing could take away the love he had within

Hung upon a cross then laid inside a tomb
And on the third day he walked out of that room
This battle has been won in all of his good works
He asks this from his heart that you love until it hurts

# Love

It's a four letter word that means so much
It's a powerful word that can really touch
You should only use it if you for sure
That the feelings you have is love so pure

Love is like a river flowing through a person's heart
You will know the feeling from the very start
When love comes puking on your heart strings
You will feel you can fly on an eagles wings

Love will carry you through all your years
Love will comfort you through all of your tears
True love is not lost and you cannot replace
True love it comes from the Father's grace

When you find love in the place in the time
You will know love from the way that it shines
With a sparkle in the eye or a smile so bright
You are filled with the love as it shines like a light

Loved ones will come and loved ones will go
But the love in your heart is how you will know
The love that we have for family and friend
Does not expire nor does love ever end

# Messiah

People coming from miles around
Standing everywhere and sitting on the ground
Looking for the Lord where can he be found
His presence is known when he is in town

He fed five thousand with praise for above
Saved the life of a woman with nothing but love
Met a woman at a well and told her she would thirst
If she didn't change her life and put him always first

He faced every demon and sent them into the sea
He welcomed the children to sit on his knee
He challenged the Pharoah and even the priest
He knelt down humbly to wash others feet

He went by himself to go and to pray
Tempted by the devil and sent him away
Approached by the soldiers and shown no fear
His followers fought back and he healed one's ear

Shackled and beaten for the good that he taught
Beaten for the people and the lost that he sought
Humiliated and crushed and nailed to a cross
His followers and family crying for their loss

He looked to the sky and with one final breathe
He asked for forgiveness and then to his death
Placed in a tomb but the stone rolled away
He rose once again on that glorious day

# More In Love

Standing on this hill
Under an old oak tree
Looking at the land
As far as the eye can see

The flowing of the river
Through the rolling hills
The beauty in this moment
The love inside fills

The birds of the sky
The fox in the den
I know my Lord provides
My life is content

Though I may struggle
And feel times of pain
Stumble on my path
Faith in you I gain

As a duck in the air
Fights the wind as it blows
He does not stress or worry
For your path he knows

The path to salvation
The path to a place
Where there is no worry
Where we find your grace

I look to the clouds
Engulfed in the sky
More in love
With my Father on High

# MOVE

You say that you're tired
And have no power
You sit around all day
Waiting for the perfect hour

The opportunities you lose
Just sitting around
Get up out of that chair
Let your feet hit the ground

No better time than now
To make the right choice
Can you hear that sound
That's the Lord's voice

Get your body moving
Get into the groove
Get the blood flow pumping
It's time for you to move

Move inside your body
Move inside your soul
Can you feel the rhythm
The Rhythm makes you whole

Throw your hands up in the air
Feel the flow of this song
The rhythm of the Lord
You just can't go wrong

One day we'll be in heaven
And hear the angel's choir
Get into the spirit
And feel the Holy Fire

# Multiply

The runners at the mark, ready set go
The race is on, the winner soon to show
The runners in a sprint, tire before too long
Forgetting that this race, is the race of a marathon

We look up at the mountain, the distance of the peak
Strength is what we need, from where do we seek
Our finances struggle, no money just to eat
Where do we turn, to help us feel complete

If we look into the word, into our own resource
Our faith will multiply the change in our live's course
Be grateful for what you have, thankful for everyday
No matter what you face, God will make the way

The strength that you need to finish this race
The power to climb while living in his grace
Your well will never dry when you give him all the praise
Every cupboard will be full in your home for all the days

The cross is in front, while the world is behind
Your future is in him, in him the love will find
Sew into the Lord, the harvest you will reap
Is greater than the world's largest harvest heap

Greater is the power, greater is the love
You will find in the father above
He will give you plenty, miracle multiplication
When every tongue confess every person every nation

# My Change

I didn't think I should be loved
I didn't think I could be trusted
For the sins I have committed
Or the times that I have lusted

The weight I carry around
The weight lays on my shoulders
The burdens of this life
Feel bigger than some boulders

I've heard of him in stories
I've heard of what he taught
The miracles he performed
The peace that he had brought

I have come to the end
Not knowing where to turn
This world has given nothing
Every bridge that I have burned

I need a bigger change
I need a brand new start
A purpose for my life
A warming of my heart

I fall down to my knees
I cry out to your name
Will you save me from this
I don't want to feel the same

This power that I feel
The weight I felt is gone
Your spirit has overcome
The change has now begun

I didn't know how to pray
You taught me what to say
You have taken over my life
I know you are the way

# My Prayer

Lord, where do I turn
Lord, where do I go
Where is my path
And how do I grow

Please hear my prayer
Please show me how
I am ready for change
Please change me now

Fill me with strength
Comfort of mind
Wisdom to know
Patience in time

I pray that your spirit
Will spread like a wind
And then in our hearts
Will growth then begin

I am no longer
A slave to this fear
My direction will come
In your voice that I hear

I take up my sword
And hold up my shield
My faith is in you
Your love is my yield

Together we'll stand
Together we'll rise
Boldly we'll speak
With fire in our eyes

# My Worth

This cloud of emotion in driving through
My vision is blurred and I can't see you
I feel alone without you near
A fight in my head against all the fear

Lost in this world alone in the dark
I need you now I need your mark
This sadness overtakes and fills up my heart
What is my purpose what is my part

I fall on my knees fold my hands so to pray
I ask that tomorrow be a better day
Will you take my hand and guide my road
Will take the weight and bare this load

Will you fill my cup until it overflows
Will you shine your light so the whole world knows
Will you heal my heart and make it whole
Will you tell me your plan so I know my roll

Even if you don't I will still believe
That my faith in you will help me achieve
I will trust you Lord here on this earth
I will listen to you when you tell me my worth

# Never Be Shaken

What is the purpose
There is for my life
The direction I'll go
In this time I'm alive

What path will I take
The road that lies ahead
A doctor or nurse
Or a lawyer instead

I've always had this feeling
To help those in need
Or go overseas
Help the children to feed

With my past in the past
And my future before
The Lord is my pilot
I could not want more

The road I have chose
Is bumpy at times
But with his guidance
I look for the signs

I will try and succeed
But first I will fail
Each time I will rise
And him I will hail

For he is my rock
And he is salvation
My fortress and I
Will never be shaken

# NEW PATH

My God my God
Where do I start
I do not have the words
I ask you to read my heart

The tears I cry
Are streaming down my face
The world is lost and broken
I think I've lost my place

I walk a lonely path
Down this empty street
No jacket on my back
Only shoes upon my feet

Mile after mile
I know not where to turn
I seek your guidance now
Teach me so I learn

I give up the control
I had over my life
I don't want to go my way
I want to feel alive

Lord I ask you please
Forgive me of my sin
No longer feeling empty
I feel the love within

The sun begins to rise
A new day has begun
Thank you to my Lord
The Father and the Son

# New Season

Another summer is gone
With the feeling of fall
Where does time go
As the leaves covering all

Nature has its time
A time to take a rest
The crops out in the field
Are ready for harvest

For everything in life
There is a time
The love in your heart
It takes you to find

A feeling of warmth
You notice inside
A glow in your face
You cannot hide

This feeling it comes
From our king on the throne
The one gone before
The love he has shown

We reap what we sow
It depends on the type
For the good of the spirit
Or for self and your hype

Which road will you choose
The narrow or the wide
One leads to destruction
The other he will guide

Put your faith in the Lord
Will all of your heart
Follow his path
A new season will start

# Not Alone

Driving on a highway
South of Sioux Falls
Open road ahead
Away from all the walls

The engine running smooth
Some cool air blowing
I look to the east
A beautiful sunrise showing

Now is the time
God and I are alone
I listen to his words
His grace that I am shown

I feel the presence of the Lord
Sitting next to me
For he is my pilot
Consumed with his mercy

I am safe in his arms
His glory I will praise
Every mile I travel
In all the coming days

I put my faith in him
My trust while I am gone
He watches my family
Makes my children strong

I know a day will come
That I will make it home
Until that day arrives
I know I'm not alone

# Not Home Yet

I wake in the morning another day is here
My head is in pain was it the liquor or beer
As I light up a smoke and pour another drink
My life falling apart almost to the brink

Why has my life turned and come down to this
Where is all my family and moments that I've missed
The voice pushing me and speaking in my ear
I know this wrong it's all lies that I hear

The one that I love is making me think
He says he still loves me with my eyes always pink
I cannot continue to go down this road
This poison in me has become a heavy load

Today I say enough and start to make a stand
With help from my friends and family with a hand
I need to believe in something more than me
No longer hide my problem but announce publicly

The first day was hard more than I could hold
I need to remember I am worth more than gold
I continue the walk and go a many mile
My head feels better with even a smile

No longer feel worthless the evil is behind
Surrounding myself with positive and kind
Today as I speak with strength and of power
I soar like an eagle no more do I cower

I am not home yet that day will arrive
But until that day I yell I am alive
Nothing will stop or come in my way
I will climb every mountain I am sober today

# Not Hopeless

I sit here on this ground
At this busy intersection
With a sign in one hand
Feeling the pain of rejection

This hunger that I feel
The pain of nothing to eat
My home is in some boxes
I live out on this street

Divorced from my wife
My children left behind
After I lost my job
Another was hard to find

But that doesn't stop me
The strength I have inside
To believe it will be better
The Lord he is my guide

I continue to hold on hope
And pray on bended knee
This situation will change
Overcome it confidently

To find myself a home
Find a job that is the start
Taking the first steps
With confidence in my heart

My situation is only that
A bump along this road
Quit carrying everything
Give Jesus all my load

Just because you feel down
Feeling a little helpless
Remember this last thing
I'm homeless, I'm not hopeless

# Not Why But Why Not

Why do we live
In a fallen world
Where people are afraid
To be a boy or a girl

Why do we tolerate
The evil or sin
The feelings we have
Or emotions within

Why do we not trust
A God that is before
Who wants to provide
Not the less but the more

Why are we afraid
In something over us
A God that is love
This Lord is a must

Why do we ask
This question every time
The unexplained happens
The acts of a crime

He is then blamed
For every little thing
The sorrow and pain that
This world will too bring

Why do we not seek
His truth And his love
Why not find peace
From the heavens above

When we change how we look
At the battles that were fought
We will notice the question is
Not Why but Why not

# One Door

When God closes one door
He opens another
To show us a path
My sister and brother

But when bad things happen
He works to make them right
Evil is to blame
As it continues to fight

Evil has come
To kill and destroy
Whether it's someone we love
Or our faith and joy

He kills the ones we love
Here in this life
A father or a son
A daughter or a wife

We will cry many tears
Of sorrow and pain
But our comfort will come
Knowing heaven is the gain

Just don't let the pain
Fill you with hate
Cause our judgement will come
When we arrive at the gate

Just live each day
With faith and peace within
And knowing a day will come
We'll see our loved ones again

# One More Day

There comes a time when we say goodbye
There comes a time when we look at the sky
And wonder where the time has gone
And wonder as our lives move on

We see the love that we once knew
The love of family that got us through
The family glue that kept us together
The family that was there through all types of weather

We aren't promised another tomorrow
We aren't promised a life without sorrow
Our past is gone and we live in today
We look to our God to show us the way

The way that he takes us may be to his home
To stand in his presence and sit by his throne
We don't know when that time could ever be
Love your family now the ones you can see

Because the day will come when we all leave this place
We will only have memories and pictures of their face
Wishes of what we wished we could say
Wish in our heart for just one more day

# Our God

Our God is a lion
And Mighty is his Roar
He is the same today
As he was before

Our Lord was led to slaughter
Like a sacrificial lamb
The creator of this world
He is The Great I Am

He rules with love and mercy
He sits upon the throne
He fights for everyone
Because we are his own

He is a jealous God
There are no Gods before
The faithful in this life
He blesses even more

Wide is the path
That leads to destruction
But narrow is the way
That guides to resurrection

The third day he was risen
He rolled away the stone
The prophecy fulfilled
The love that he had shown

He will be coming back
For all those who believe
In paradise we will live
The gift that we receive

# Our Lord Is Alive

He came as a baby
He grew into a man
He sat with the sinners
Healed the sick with his hand

People traveled miles
To listen to him speak
He taught in the temple
Gave strength to weak

He fed five thousand
Restored sight to the blind
He walked through the desert
To help every kind

He was called a teacher
Some called him a master
He is the prince of peace
He is the pastor of pastors

He was sent for a purpose
To give his life for our sin
To rise from the grave
The new covenant to begin

Beaten like a slave
And hung on a tree
In the most brutal ways
Anyone could ever be

Death thought it won
But faith did revive
The stone rolled away
Our Lord is alive

## Our Place

There is this mystery
An unsolved story
We hear of this man
Who is the glory

In the papers written
Is told he is king
Who is this man
Who holds everything

He is a gift to many
A new peace for all
His life that is given
Is stronger than a wall

Samaritan or Egyptian
Gentile or Jew
He comes for us all
And not just a few

There is no secret
Our God and his love
The son that he sent
Is more than enough

The veil has been torn
Our Lord has arrived
The promise is kept
His life glorified

He has gone before
He knows what's to come
He lives within us
We are filled with the son
Filled with his power
We are filled with his grace
Given his strength
By his side is our place

# Pandemic

The door flew open and the new year entered
Good was pushed aside and evil became centered
Man against man lies became good
Fear consumed many like no other could

Shelves were empty social media was not
Media spread fear while the fire burned hot
Eyes were shut to the things that are right
The voice of the many weak in the fight

Churches were closed and pastors arrested
The teacher is quiet while we are all tested
Push aside the fear cast your eyes to the Lord
Take up all the armour along with your sword

Meditate in the word refuel in his power
His time will come so prepare for the hour
Recharge for today be full for tomorrow
Get into his grace and his will is to follow

We need to become lovers of all
Bring every color of human together for this call
Spreading the word in the street and the land
Singing his praise heart to heart hand to hand

Even on this day Jesus remains on the throne
He hears all your prayers you are not alone
Fall to your knees your hands in the air
A new day has come for his children everywhere

# Passion

Born to a virgin a carpenter by trade
Known by his teaching and the footsteps he made
He cared for the lepers gave sight to the blind
He said he was searching for his sheep that he would find

A threat to the kingdom that men built in the land
Faithful to his believers and the sick he helped stand
He did not stress or worry for food or a bed
He fed a lot of people with fish and some bread

He was tested by the priests and accused of blasphemy
He did not hide the miracles he wanted everyone to see
Tempted by the devil while he prayed on the mount
Kindness and love is what his teaching was about

Taken in the night with a kiss he was betrayed
Denied by a brother after promises were made
He endured so much pain no man could survive
After three days he said he'd be alive

Put on a cross and left there to die
He prayed for the people lifted his eyes to the sky
Placed in a tomb and wrapped in a sheet
With scars in his wrists and holes in his feet

Just as he promised when the third day was done
The stone rolled away a light brighter than the sun
He stepped from the tomb death is defeated
His name is Jesus Christ and next to the father he is seated

He did this for you he did this for all
He's calling your name so answer the call
He is waiting and knocking on the door of your heart
A relationship with him forgiveness is the start

# PATIENCE

Are you feeling tired and weak
Feeling a little down
It's hard to even smile
All day you wear a frown

You fall down to your knees
And cry out through your tears
You feel that your prayers
Have fallen on deaf ears

Do not fret my daughter
Do not fear my son
The Lord is with you
And the war has been won

Have patience my child
And believe you will stand
One day in his kingdom
At the Lord's right-hand

Have patience in the work
Have patience with the other
We are all from one God
We are all sister and brother

This life is a story
A beautiful work of art
The author is our father
Who loves all from his heart

Hold on a little longer
And one day you will see
That you create a masterpiece
Patience is the key

# Plug In

I'm sitting in darkness
I search of some light
The electricity is off
As I continue to fight

A greatness I seek
A greatness in power
When will it come
When is the hour

Then I heard your word
Your strong holy voice
Telling me to speak
Telling me to rejoice

Rejoice I his word
And speak over bones
Bring life to the dead
And spread to the homes

But God I am not you
No power to give life
He stopped me right then
With a great and bright light

He put in my heart
The words now to say
A way to plug in
To his power today

Plug in to the Christ
A solution you will find
Electricity you need
The power of his kind

# Priceless

You may have a chipped tooth
Or a funny haircut
Be the tallest in your class
Overweight with a little gut

Thick rimmed glasses
Not wearing designer clothes
You don't have the latest phone
Or watch the trending shows

Your shoes don't cost a lot
You drive a beat up car
Your house is not a mansion
I will tell you something you are

You are loved and beautiful
Your worth is more than gold
You're priceless in God's eyes
The love your heart does hold

It doesn't matter what you have
It doesn't matter how you look
Your story isn't finished
A masterpiece of a book

To others you may look weak
What you see in the mirror after a shower
The weight you feel each day
Remember knowledge is power

Keep helping others
Be a shining star
You are an important person
In life you will go far

# Psalm 1

Blessed be the man
Whose faith is in God
Who walks in the right
The narrow path he has trod

He sits not in the seat
Of the scorned and the sin
He standeth in the way
Of the evil within

He delights in the law
Meditates day and night
Planted like a tree
He will flourish in the light

Next to rivers of water
His seed will great
His leaf will not wither
In the season of late

The ungodly like a chaff
That the wind blows away
Will not stand with the right
They do not follow the Lord's say

The ungodly will perish
The Lord knoweth the way
With every setting of the sun
And the start of each day

# Psalm 28

Unto you I will cry
Oh Lord you are my rock
You are the mighty shepherd
I am missing from the flock

I ask to hear your voice
Be not silent to me
I lift my arms to heaven
I seek guidance from the holy

I am lost among the wicked
Release me from this hell
The iniquity of these workers
The corruption that they sell

They regard not the works
Nor the operation of his hands
He will not build them up
But destroy where evil stands

Blessed be the Lord
Because he hath heard my voice
He is my strength and shield
In him I made my choice

I rejoice with my heart
I will praise him with my song
My faith is found in him
His anointed is made strong

I ask this of my Lord
To save and feed his sheep
To lift the anointed up
The inheritance we will keep

# Put Off

The wicked run
When no one is
Stand strong where you are
No matter what you're facing

Do not run
It may seem strange
But God has a time
A time for a change

The times of the past
Are long left and gone
Now is the moment
Your life will move on

Change your life for the good
As Christ would have done
He faced every change
And never would have run

Put off your old clothes
The ones filled with sin
Take up your cleanliness
And his grace is within

Christ came to give us life
the way you are going
Receive what he gives you
And the love he is showing

Take the truth that he brings
And the word he has told
Believe in his love
You're more valuable than gold

# Ready For The Ride

I can see the horizon
I have an open road
Have everything I need
My bible is my load

Nothing holding me back
I'm ready for the ride
Ready for this path
Taking it in stride

The Lord is my pilot
He is my guiding light
I will not be in want
He's my strength in this fight

Bible in my hand
My heart is filled with grace
Comfort in the knowing
His love has filled this place

The world will try it's best
To hurt and knock me down
But faith inside my heart
I'm protected by the crown

I'll go from town to town
Teaching of the word
To share the gospel stories
And the truth that I have heard

And when my ride is done
The joy I'll feel inside
So when the next time arrives
I'll be ready for the ride

# Relationships

With dirty clothes
And unkept hair
The gifts he gives
Calls us to share

To share the love
Share with each other
Whether they are
Our sister or our brother

Life is not meant
To live it alone
Build a relationship
His love to be shown

A relationship starts
When you extend your hand
Welcoming the other
Next to them you stand

Spreading his word
Sharing love with each other
Supporting the young
Like a father or mother

Some will be hard
Hard in the heart
Not want to listen
As their life falls apart

Words will be hard
Just talk with your heart
Speak through the Lord
The building will then start

# Return To The Word

Questions we ask
The answers to know
Which direction to turn
Which way should we go

With lessons to learn
Temptation overcome
Steps on our path
The word we learn from

The beginning of a story
The story for everyone
Instructions for this life
Finished by the son

So why do we rebel
Live life on our own
More faith in ourselves
With pride we go alone

Are we greater than others
With all that we know
Evolution is believed
No proof have to show

We need to be humbled
The pride will destroy
Open the bible
Find the peace and the joy

Bring life to a pace
His voice can be heard
Give over control
And return to the word

# Servant To Others

The ground is plowed and ready for seed
But there is so much more this ground will need
Someone to water and pull out the weed
Prepare for a harvest and the mouths it will feed

The ground is the church the place we call home
The place that we go so we are not alone
Fellowship and love of Christ will be shown
The place that our ancestors have been and grown

The church needs the servant who works to cultivate
The servants who make an experience great
Those who will water and help in your fight
And those who will love and shine his great light

The church is the place for the sick not the well
To help you get up because you just fell
Volunteer of your time and feed the homeless
Look at the world and see who we can bless

Just as soldiers have a mission in war
The mission of the church is to open a door
The door to salvation and grace through his love
The door to the path to God up above

Do it not for yourself but to God who provides
Stand up and serve until the darkness hides
The light of the Lord covers every corner of earth
Every person will see in the Lord their own worth

Connect with the world connect with each other
Reach out to your fellow sister and brother
Embrace the Lord's vision of serving in this time
Like the sun on a field that continues to shine

# She Is A Mother

She is chosen by God to lead the way
She is strong in the mind each and every day
Tried and tested but patient in the heart
Courage of a lion from the very start

Kindness and comfort like the holy lamb
She drops everything she's doing whenever she can
She picks you up and wipes away tears
She takes you in her arms and takes away your fears

A single mother or one married to a man
She is the one the family needs to stand
So remember the sacrifice your mother has made
The sleepless nights to help you make the grade

A teacher of every subject in school
A lifeguard to protect you from falling in the pool
A chauffeur to drive you to every activity
She'd give you her last dollar because of generosity

If your mother is living or she has passed
Remember them this day for everything they were asked
Tell her you love because you won't get another
Hold her close to your heart she is a mother

# Shed A Tear

Today is the day
I shed a tear
A tear out of sorrow
And not out of fear

A tear for a father
A tear for a son
A tear for a daughter
A mother of one

No matter the person
Their fortune or fame
They were all loved by some
They all had a name

A nurse who cares
A soldier who serves
A farmer who tends
With the calmest of nerves

A trucker who drives
An athlete who plays
No matter the person
They value their days

So when there's an accident
And lives that are lost
Hold dear in our hearts
There is more that was cost

Each life is valued
No life is worth more
We remember each person
And their life gone before

# Show Them The Way

Born as a baby we come into this world
Grow into a child a boy or a girl
The years go by and time disappears
Our bodies change rapidly as a teenager nears

Before we know it we graduate from school
Thrown into a place with nothing but a tool
The next step we take will effect what's to come
New places and adventures much different than where we're from

Get married become parents as we make the choice
The new addition comes and it's time to rejoice
Our lives will change as a mom or a dad
Need to teach them the way the good and the bad

You will make mistakes you will continue to fall
You will face a mountain but you must make the call
The call that will help and show them to climb
The call that you stand and will get through this time

When you lead they will follow
What you do it will show
Be a thermostat to change the environment around
Show them the Lord and their path that is bound

If you have question or any other concern
Just listen for his voice and you will soon learn
Be for your children like has does for you
Show them the way and all of the love too.

# Signs Of

There are feelings you have
That you're wrestling with inside
The emotions that you have
Are getting harder to hide

The years gone by
Struggling with it alone
Fighting each day
Will the end ever be shown

I wake up each day
Fearing of what's to come
Pushing through this weakness
Where will my strength come from

Each day in this life
There are signs I have seen
That stop me in the moment
But what do they mean

Signs of my path
Signs of this road
Signs of my sorrow
And signs of this load

I have come to time
I have fallen to my knees
I have cried out to heaven
Will the Lord hear my pleas

The next day I wake
I feel a great release
Just trust in the Lord
And he will bring you peace

# Solid Ground

You make the winning shot
In a basketball game
Instantly made famous
Everyone knows your name

Your name goes up in lights
And everywhere you go
People shout your name
Even strangers you don't know

The fame that you now have
Creates an ego in your head
The spotlights are on you
You love yourself instead

This will only last a time
And then you'll feel alone
The lesson you will learn
You reap just what you've sewn

No matter what you have
It will not be enough
To provide a happiness
Just pleasure from your stuff

You need to humble yourself
Rid your life of pride
And then you'll start to feel
A change you need inside

The walls will start to fall
No longer you surround
You feel a brand new freedom
Your feet on solid ground

# STAY IN MY LANE

Looking at this path and the direction I came
Searching for greatness in fortune and fame
Building my place in behind these walls
Shutting out the people and all of their calls

In this little world I live in right now
There is no one greater that I need to bow
I built my own kingdom right here in this lane
But I still feel sadness along with the pain

What did I do where did I go wrong
Why does it feel that this path is so long
I need someone greater to carry this load
I need more direction to keep me on the road

I need to stay in this lane you've chosen for me
Put your name in lights for everyone to see
Give you all the glory for your kingdom
And tear down walls of my own thingdom

Because straight is the gate and narrow the way
I give up myself to follow you today
Please take my hand in you I will gain
I will prosper in life as I stay in my lane

# Step Of Faith

Growing up as a child
We had made some choices
Things to prove ourselves
Giving into the voices

The older we grew
Some choices we made
Were better than before
As our youth starts to fade

We look at those times
We believed in ourself
Not looking to others
For advice or for help

But now in this time
I know there is something
That is greater than I
He is great as a king

I have learned of his love
A love he has for me
He fights for my life
With his grace and mercy

He is bold in his love
And mighty is his name
His voice can move mountains
My life will never be the same

I take this step of faith
Bold faith in his word
It strengthens my life
The greatest ever heard

# That Place

What does it profit
A man to gain
Material things
The world or fame

A painted portrait
Or your name in lights
Thousands of followers
Or Facebook likes

None of it matters
When we leave this earth
We came to this world
With nothing at Birth

Joy is not found
In the things we possess
Just the love that we share
And the truth we profess

The money we have
Can be taken away
It will not keep us warm
Or buy happiness each day

Happiness comes
From a place in the heart
A place we have had
From a very early start

Look inside your heart
And you will find that place
Filled with flowing love
Mercy and his grace

# The Beginning

Some say he is God
Others claim he is not
The truth of his life
Is not to be forgot

The trinity is the truth
That all three are one
The story that was written
Is when the truth begun

The time the world follows
Does not explain his life
Before and after Christ
He was there the whole time

When the world began
Christ was on the throne
Creating every life
From our heavenly home

He is the glue that holds
All things together
Not for a short time
The glue that lasts forever

All things were created
Through him and him alone
He gave us a purpose
Through him our purpose shown

He is the head of all
The start of every word
From the beginning to today
The truth must be heard

We must follow him closely
So others will follow too
Teach the world that we know
That world will become new

# The Call

God chose David
The weakest of them all
To stand against a giant
To answer his call

Moses had a stutter
A problem with his speech
But he had heard the call
Guided people from beach to beach

Daniel was a prophet
In captivity he was taken
And with a faith in God
He survived the lions' den

Daniel had some friends
Who were thrown into the fire
With faith that could move mountains
Were saved by a God that's higher

Chosen for a purpose
These men answered the call
The least of the many
Chosen from them all

The weak that are not strong
Or problems while you speak
God doesn't use the righteous
He uses the very meek

So come out of the shadows
Standing faithful and tall
Get ready for the moment
The moment to answer the call

# The Choice

The people are full
And covered in sin
They live their lives
Being empty within

They follow the belief
That they need more than him
More than the Christ
To succeed with a win

But God sends a man
One to be heard
To teach what they need
And the meaning of his word

Those who have more
And material is taught
Need to inventory life
In this world they fought

Following discipline
Follow self-control
Seek out the Christ
He will make you whole

Renew in your life
And humble yourself
Drop to your knees
And call out for help

He hears what you say
He wipes away sins
Your blood will flow clean
Your new life begins

We take from this day
In the future we will rejoice
From the decisions that were made
And you made the choice

# The Climb

I pulled out the list
That started as a dream
The list has gotten smaller
From when I was a teen

What can we do
What can we accomplish
Then I remembered the thousands
Fed with bread and some fish

At one time I heard
The voice of the one
Who discourages and says
This cannot be done

A stronger voice was heard
With comfort and peace
Believe in the Christ
Who strengthens your needs

I made the call
To follow the voice
That gives me the peace
And in him I rejoice

This mountain is tall
And hard to climb
Others have tried
And failed many time

But my God told me
No valley too low
No mountain to high
His grace cannot go

People to support
Along this way
Stand beside me
On this glorious day

I start the climb
My way to the top
My faith is strong
I will not stop

I have struggled
And sometimes fell
But God picked me up
And helped me excel

A push in the back
A still small voice
Well done my child
You made the right choice

Up on this mountain
Is where I now stand
And look at the beauty
Our God who is grand

# The Fight

Babies being killed
And riots breaking out
The evil is growing
With a thunderous shout

Revelations has told
Of the days yet to come
Of the wars being started
And the falling of some

A war that is fought
Not with guns or with knives
But with words used to hurt
And destroy all the lives

The weapon that is used
Is a weapon filled with hate
This weapon doesn't care
If your white, gay or straight

It divides all the people
Against one another
And builds a great wall
Between a sister and a brother

We call on you Lord
For the greatest of tools
The strength that you have
To fight all the fools

This tool that you have
Is the tool filled with love
A love like no other
The love from above

We will once again win
This fight that is inside
With Christ in our hearts
The evil will then hide

# The Fisherman

His boat is launched into the lake
How much time will it take
Before he gets his first fish
Very soon is all he can wish

He cast his net into a spot
Just like his father before had taught
The day goes by with nothing to see
He pulls his net and continues to worry

A man approaches and gets in his boat
Who is this man what does he know
He tells the man there are no fish
Jesus says give me time and I will fulfill your wish

Cast your net in the place I say
Just believe in me and have some faith
The nets were filled and almost broke
With his eyes wide open the fisherman is woke

Jesus told him leave everything behind
Follow me and men we will find
I will use you throughout the land
A common person you will stand

Give a man a fish he eats for a day
Show him to fish you will show him my way
Now go into the world and teach them to pray
And you will be the change that we need today

# The Fuel

A candle sits
In a window sill
The flame does flicker
With a room to fill

Its size is small
Not very strong
But the light it gives
Does carry on

The flame you see
Is like in your heart
A flame that's burnt
From the very start

What do we need
To make it grow
Where is the fuel
For the flame to show

The fuel has a name
His name is Christ
He will fill up your tank
With a wonderful light

Fill up the space
That's empty inside
With the strength he gives
The love will not hide

Your flame will be strong
Like a grassland wildfire
The fuel that we need
The way we become higher

He is our rock
Our salvation we stand
We are his army
And we fight for his land

# The God of Forever

The storm clouds and the thunder rolls
The wind is blowing and the flood water flows
A ship that tosses as the waters crash
How will this end as my life begins to flash

As the storm rages and my heart fills with fear
What can I do and my voice will you hear
In the eye of the storm the clouds begin to part
And I feel a great light that shines on my heart

He whispers to me in a still and small voice
He tells to trust and in him to rejoice
He has seen the outcome and cares for you friend
The alpha and omega the beginning and end

Fill your hearts with faith and praise his name
Lose all the fear and the panic the same
He will rebuke all the wind and calm every sea
Fall on your face or bow every knee

He is the God of today tomorrow and forever
He is over all things over here or wherever
He is greater than the world everything every man
All things under his authority he has a plan

When we are lost and fighting the waves
He is like a lighthouse for ships it saves
He cares not your past yesterday is null
He looks for those that will stand faithful

You don't need a life raft when he is in control
He is our healer he will make is whole
Get out of the boat that's sinking in sin
His kingdom is offered and wants you within

Go forth from this day a witness for God
Testify to others every road that you trod
    In Jesus Christ the rock I stand
    All other ground is sinking sand

# The Great Catch

The anchor is cast the nets are strung
You hold onto hope until the work is done
Patience is the key for the greater things
The riches of the Lord is what patience brings

When you rush your time in every day
You will miss the chance to show the way
Have faith inside that you will keep
And cast your nets into the deep

It's not the fish that you will seek
But the heart of man the weary the weak
Work to change the heart that's full of sin
Have faith in God for the change to begin

The net is just a word that is used
For the love God has for the sinfully accused
Love is the greatest of tools
Love is needed to reach all of the fools

The fish are just those who are lost
Those who are dumb to the Lord's true cost
So cast his love into the sea
His great catch is what will be

Evil will not win over his great love
Found not on this earth but his kingdom above
Rise up now and listen to his word
Cast your net until everyone has heard

# The Greatest

This world is filled
With material things
Money and lust
And the sins that it brings

Lovers of self
Haters of others
We judge all the people
Even sisters and brothers

Not afraid to do harm
To most in this world
With deceit in our hearts
And the lies that are hurled

Look down upon most
Cause we don't see their worth
We build up our empires
Try to rule over the earth

But it can all be gone
With the swipe of a hand
Destroyed in a heartbeat
No life on this land

We should listen to the Lord
And the words that he spoke
Just open our eyes
To a world that is broke

Start following the teacher
And his teachings in whole
Love the Lord your God
With heart, mind and soul

# The Harvest

The seed has been planted
In the ground of the fields
The planter now knows
The wait for the yields

He is not impatient
Because he knows if he is
He can lose all the gain
And the time will he miss

The same goes for those
Who sew in our God
The response is not instant
Like the seed in the sod

When we sew in the Lord
It will not be done
Right there in the moment
His work just begun

He wants much for you
You reap what you sew
You give from the heart

In the love you will know
Keep faith in our God
And open the door
The harvest is coming
Abundance galore

# The Lantern

The darkness consumes
In this ongoing fight
No matter what we do
We cannot see the light

We pray from our knees
Not knowing if he hears
Consumed by the loneliness
Overtaken by our fears

What can we do
Which way can we turn
To open our eyes
What do we learn

And then a still small voice
Is heard in the night
Telling of his plan
Of his strength and his might

Light your lantern
With a fire
Give power to your prayer
Let me take you higher

Every day while awake
In the calm and the storm
On the mountain and the valley
More faith you will form

Take this lantern where you go
I will guide you in the truth
Use the ears that you have
Have gratitude too

Being proactive in this day
And praising in his name
This day going forward
Your name he will claim

# The Last Drop

The last drop of water
The last grain of sand
The sun no longer shines
Men and women no longer stand

Death and war prevail
The enemy comes to destroy
To rob the blessed and happy
To kill any ounce of joy

But one is soon to come
Who is greater than the earth
Visions have been seen
And revelations since his birth

His name is the Christ
The risen son of God
Who brings peace and love
Everywhere that he will trod

After seven years of war
Is a thousand years of love
Everyone will be your brother
Like heaven from above

Deserts no longer dry
Waters will be clean
Animals live together
Like never before seen

Be prepared this time to come
It will arrive like a thief in the night
Don't wait til the last second
To accept his guiding light

# The Memories

Rough on the outside
But the softest of hearts
Strength to move mountains
Before the day even starts

The guidance of a father
With the gentlest hand
Will protect you from danger
When you fall help you stand

When we need advice
For the times when they come
You told us not to stop
Until the job has been done

And now we look back
On the times that we had
The hugs that we shared
The good and the bad

We will ask why
As we shed some tears
But yet we are thankful
For the days and the years

The memories we made
The times that we had
We hold you close to our heart
We will miss you dad

# The New Life

Murder in the streets destruction in the land
People turning to drugs not believing they can stand
Pain in their hearts blood on the ground
The enemy leaves a wake of hate that's spread around

Turning brother against brother
Turning daughter against mother
What can we do to save this planet earth
When our future is being killed by abortion before birth

Will someone stand up let their voice be loud
Get the attention of all that spread into the crowd
One has come before who died upon a cross
He died in our place and paid an expensive cost

And on the third day he had rose again
To give us hope we need to show us we will win
Open up your heart he's knocking on the door
He will show you love and pain will be no more

Hope in everlasting life is what he will provide
Hope that things can change if you let him come inside
Broken will be fixed the hungry will be fed
The sick will be healed the lost will be led

Because he has been risen he defeated death
We will continue living even after our last breathe
He is the promise that we will live again
Give your heart to him and the new life will begin

# The Prayer

The leaves are changing with a chill in the air
A new season is coming for all everywhere
We will not be afraid of the times that will come
We are faithful and know where our strength comes from

    Fill our hearts with your presence Lord
    Protect us Lord from the enemy's sword
    His wicked tongue with lies and deceit
    He summons his army to fill every street

But we look to the meadow and notice a tree
The almond tree with a new beginning we'll see
    Come to us Lord take away all the dead
    Let your mercy rain all over our head

Just like you took the sick and made whole
Have your way in our life and fill our soul
We yield to your presence please come to this place
    We bow at your presence and fall on our face

    We ask you Lord not to put us on a stage
    Put your name in lights right now in this age
    We ask for the patience we need in this time
    We know you supply every dollar and dime

We mount up like eagles and soar through the sky
    Your power will heal in your arms we lie
We pray in your name and know even when
    Your love is amazing we thank you Amen

# The Reason

The lights are on the house
New snow is on the ground
The stores are filled with cheer
A bustle through the town

The time of year has come
With presents under the tree
Families traveling miles
Loved ones for to see

People in many nations
Celebrate this time of year
Giving gifts to show their love
To family far and near

But we should not forget
The greatest gift of all
Was born in a lonely manger
A trough in a cattle stall

A king became a baby
Grew up to be a man
He taught the word of God
The best way any can

He gave up greater things
A throne and a better life
Because he loves all people
He took the pain and strife

So remember when you celebrate
This Christmas and this season
A king came to this world
And Jesus is the reason

# The Rose

For every season
There comes a time
A time your heart's
True love to find

A time to grow
Just like the rose
A time for love
Your heart only knows

The rain will fall
From time to time
But a rose will wait
For the sun to shine

Be patient and kind
Your love will grow strong
Faithful to the other
Together you belong

God has chosen you
To share in this life
Be joined at the heart
A husband to his wife

The path that you walk
Holding the other's hand
Will feel at times rough
But together you stand

You are no longer two
But two become one
Joined by a love
That can't be undone

# The Star

The prophecy told
Of a star in the night
Foretold by the prophets
That will shine very bright

The prophecy states
In the east of the sky
The star will arise
With a path from up high

The path that they speak
Is paved for a king
This king will be born
As a celestial chorus sings

Some people thought
This king is a man
Who will save all the people
And take over the land

What they didn't know
A baby to be born
Will save all the people
And the land that is torn

Caesar set out
To kill every child
To save his own kingdom
And rule with a wild

Then Jesus was born
A king in the night
As the star shined above
With the Lord's guiding light

# The Stars

The stars that sparkle
Up in the night sky
They shine On The world
From very up high

They teach us a lesson
No matter how dark
It is in our life
There's always a spark

We can sparkle and shine
Our brightest each day
To teach all the lost
That he is the way

He is the truth
And he is the life
The king of all kings
The bringer of light

The prince of peace
A teacher to all
In your time of need
His name you can call

Just listen for his voice
Any place any time
A whisper in the wind
His grace you will find

His mercy abundant
His love is abound
The Lord of this world
In our hearts he is found

# The Tongue

The word that was spoken
To create the whole earth
Was the same word spoken
To create you before birth

From the moment you were born
A word was the start
From the breathe that you took
To the beat of your heart

The power of the tongue
Has the power to kill
The power to create
Through the speaking of his will

Don't give the enemy
The power that you've got
Speak only the positive
And erase the word not

Believe in your heart
And speak that you can
Believe that you will
Believe the great I am

In order for a harvest
You must plant the seed
Believe in our God
He will supply what you need

He does not call the qualified
He qualifies the called
Just trust in his faithfulness
Even when your life feels stalled

Find patience in the Lord
Find strength in the word
Just silence your tongue
And his voice will be heard

# THE VINE

Our God in the beginning created the light
The moon to mirror and shine in the night
The wind to blow the pollen and seed
The rivers winding into the ocean they feed

He provides the worm for the birds to eat
The grass in the meadow for the cattle to treat
So why do you stress when problems arise
He knows the place of the stars in the skies

You are not just a number He knows you by name
He cares about you not your riches or fame
The creator of all everything in this world
Every beast of the field every boy every girl

He is the vine from which we will grow
Before we even pray our needs he does know
On Christ the solid rock I stand
All other ground is sinking sand

He is our strength our might power
Watching over us in every hour
Faithful to love and faithful to give
In Christ alone is where we should live

# The Voice

Someone once told me
That I was too small
Someone once told me
I wouldn't matter at all

Someone once told me
That I was too thin
Someone once told me
That I wouldn't win

Someone once told me
That I wasn't smart
But what they don't know
Is the size of my heart

As I look in the mirror
At the one looking at me
More strength and more courage
Is what I do see

I see a man
That stands at my side
A man that is love
That he does not hide

I know that I can
I will and I am
No longer afraid
On his love I will stand

The voice that I hear
Is confident and strong
A belief in myself
As I carry on

# Their Part

From the jungles of Vietnam
To the deserts of Iraq
Some served during peacetime
To prevent an enemy attack

Sailing the way on the seas
Rushing in like a marine
Flying high in the clouds
Or wearing all Army green

They made an oath to the people
Wrote a check that was blank
To serve in the deepest
Or be stuck in a tank

Remember their face
Remember their name
They wish to be humble
They don't look for fame

They will say it's their job
It's what's in their heart
It's their mark in this life
Their way to do their part

# This Old Wooden Cross

Weathered and worn from an old oak tree
Cut and used as punishment for all to see
The timbers connected with a piece of rope
Little did they know this cross would become hope

These pieces of wood just thrown at his feet
Made to carry the cross through the city street
Too heavy to carry by any ordinary man
He was forced to carry this cross until he couldn't stand

Stained with his blood and soaked in his sweat
No one in the crowd knew the harder it would get
The wood that he laid on was meant to build a home
Not for Christ our Lord to die on there alone

As it was planted in the ground
With his accusers standing around
He hung there on that cross until his final breathe
He said that it is finished before he entered death

Death could not contain as he rose to life again
A sacrificial lamb and new life to begin
So remember when you see this old wooden cross
God gave us his son to save us from the loss.

# This Weight

This weight I have
Upon my shoulders
Feels like the weight
Of a thousand boulders

This feels like I'm sinking
In the middle of a lake
No life vest to grab
Or a hand I can take

Overwhelmed by an avalanche
Of snow on this hill
Overtaken by the power
I pray for your will

Your will to be released
From the shackles on me
The chains on my wrists
I want to be free

Free from this pain
That I feel everyday
I search for the sun
To enlighten my way

Only one has the power
To release all the pain
Only one loves so much
To give you the gain

Just reach out to him
Cry his name in the night
He is waiting for the moment
To shine down his light

# Through Me

Magic fairy dust
Or riches of the earth
Neither will save your life
Or change your very worth

The money in your bank
Possessions in your home
The clothes upon your back
The newest model of phone

Cars inside your garage
Your status in this life
Won't amount to much
When you leave this life and die

Before your final day
Before the end of light
There is a way to save
Your soul against this fight

Born on Christmas day
This child that is a king
He came from heaven above
You could hear the angels sing

He lived his life to serve
He traveled miles to preach
A guide of how to live
And lessons he would teach

No matter what you have
Possessions you may see
No one comes to the father
Unless you come through me

# Time For A Change

Been feeling alone
Tired and lost
Which way to turn
My life the cost

Isolated in life
Stuck in these walls
Alone I this jungle
Not hearing my calls

No fellowship to feel
Is this what I miss
When will the door open
This is my wish

Tear down these walls
I want to be free
Out of this jungle
So I can then see

The words that are said
And the words that are wrote
Can lift a man up
In the way they are spoke

The walls coming down
It seems really bright
A warm gentle voice
Leading me in light

It's time for a change
No more being alone
It's time for a change
I now feel at home

# TIME

Each person has a life
Each life there is a purpose
Each person needs to find
The reason in this circus

Each day goes by too fast
Each month and year are gone
Our children are all grown
Our lives don't seem so long

But we must slow it down
Before we lose the time
We are missing all the beauty
That God gave us to find

Stop to watch the stars
Or watch the day's sunset
Some things can just wait
For the moments that we get

The world is filled with noise
Created to distract
We need to turn our ears
And better ways to react

Paradise is before us
A better world to have
Stop and see the love
The beauty in the land

So take this moment now
Give your family time
Enjoy our Father's gifts
And love you will then find

# Today Is The Day

You treated me as weak
You treated me as low
I am not an animal
I am human you know

You tore me down
And made me cry
You pushed me down
With no reason why

Let me tell you this
I'll tell you this way
Things are going to change
Because today is the day

Today is the day
I stand on my two feet
Today is the day
I kick you to the street

Today is the day
I get my life back
Today is the day
You no longer can attack

Today is the day
I say I am someone
Today is the day
I say that I have won

Today is the day
I get strength over you
Today is the day
My life becomes brand new

You've had a second chance
And even a third
Today is the day
My voice will be heard

# TOGETHER

We live in a world that is terribly broken
The hate that we hear and the words that are spoken
Color vs color and man vs man
We try to overcome with everything that we can

We need to be heard when we march in the street
Do like Dr. King had done with his feet
We must not live by all separate color
Learn to love our neighbor as we love one another

Blacks with the whites the yellow and red
Save every life of our children before they're dead
Someday we will leave to go live in peace
Every father and daughter uncle and niece

Starting today we must make a stand
And look at the heart not the color of the hand
Every man woman and child every tribe every tongue
We will not see peace until the Lord's song is sung

Together we stand divided we fall
Our hearts joined as one we will answer the call
The only color seen is the color of love
We are made in the image of our Father above

# Until The End

I live my own life
With kindness to all
From the day that I started
And answered the call

Humility and integrity
Are only a few
Of the gifts I received
In my life thanks to you

The God of the people
The King to all men
Your grace and your love
Complete til the end

You've called me to stand
Take the field once more
I call on your strength
As I walk through this door

Move to a new city
Be part of a team
Every play that I make
I exalt unto thee

Until the last whistle
And the game is all done
No matter the score
It is you who has won

# Until We Meet Again

Our time in this world will come to an end
When we leave behind our family and friends
We will go to a place not far away
Where there is no night just forever day

There will be no sorrow or pain we'll feel
Just a peaceful feeling with love so real
And when I go I ask you this
Do not cry for the times you'll miss

Know that where I am is in the father's hands
Because I lived by his will and his plans
Please use my body to help the world
Whoever needs a kidney a boy or a girl

Eyes to see or a heart to live
Are the least of me I want to give
Material things will come and go
But my love to you I want you to know

Each passing day with the rising sun
Keep fighting the fight until the war is won
A gentle breeze of springtime day
The smell of the flowers in the month of May

I will be with you as the moon shines down
In the songs of the birds in the trees of your town
It is not forever I have gone to a place
I will see you again in our Lord's heavenly grace

# Vision of Missions

Numerous countries across thousands of miles
Tribes on land and people in the isles
Have never experienced or ever heard
The love of Christ or guidance in the word

Christ on earth had such a great vision
A vision to spread his word through a mission
All of the disciples were given such a power
A power to preach and prepare them for the hour

To reach the sinners and find all the lost
Pray continuously even if their life is the cost
Tell others of the day when Christ will return
Teach them the ways and the word they should learn

Saving the lives in foreign lands
Being Christ's heart and his healing hands
The vision of mission is bringing life to the dead
Curing diseases from their toes to their head

We are being called to be salt and the light
Suit up with your armor get ready for the fight
The fight for good the fight for their soul
When they are brought to the light Christ will make them whole
So put on your coat and strap on your boots
Get to work for the Lord and put down some roots
Humble yourselves and give in to submission
Your work starts today in the field in the mission

# WALK BY FAITH

In a blinding snowstorm, I will walk by faith
In the dark of night, I will walk by faith
I will walk by faith, and not by sight
When no one is watching, I will do what's right

Some believe because they have seen
Others walk in ways that they believe
You have faith when you're in your car
You have faith when you travel far

How is that different than having faith in God
How is that different than the faith you've got
Let go of the things you have in this world
In his eyes you are greater than a pearl

More valuable than a diamond left in the rough
When we are down he will lift us up
He is the God of miracles and works unseen
He forgives our sins and wipes us clean

When something happens the world has no answer
They look to science in a worldly matter
They take away from the power he has
But will be left with nothing when the world does pass

I believe in miracles I believe in his plan
I believe in miracles and all that he can
I will walk by faith In my life everyday
I will choose the path chosen for his way

What do you have what can you lose
To believe in a God his work will he prove
Miracles still happen in the world In his way
Open your eyes and you will see them today

# WE PRAY

What is your name what is your story
Why do you care why do you worry
Who do you follow who do you align
When will you change when is your time

Your time is now for change to come
You follow The Lord his kingdom you're from
A heart for all my sisters and brothers
My name is child of the creator of others

I am made new and stronger than before
I will walk through the fire and fear no more
I will stand on the rock and not on the sand
Walking the path while he holds my hand

Before I was broken but know I am whole
I give up my life for him to take control
As for my family we will serve the Lord
I am the protector of this home we afford

The Lord will supply according to his riches
His word and his presence our lives it enriches
He's calling all men to stand in his word
Every nation and color his voice will be heard

The lost and the found the strong and the meek
When he calls our name any day of the week
We will step forward like a soldier in war
We love one another not hate like before

Our criminal acts are left in the past
The veil is torn like the lowering of a mast
Men of a God who lives still today
We fall to our knees and together we pray

A house divided cannot stand
A country will fall with hate in the land
We can overcome with love in our heart
We must turn now to God for the start

# We Stand

The colors of the rainbow
Are all different hues
Just like the people
That God's going to use

He does not value
One over another
A man or a woman
A sister or a brother

No matter where they live
The country or the land
Created in his image
Created hand in hand

We stand for the Lord
We search for the lost
We fight for each other
No matter the cost

No borders can stop
The spread of your love
To show that all people
Fit like a hand to a glove

When we are called home
We don't need a reservation
In our God's kingdom
We are all of one nation

So, tear down the walls
And speak to every ear
Reach out to every heart
And witness with no fear

# WHAT IF I

What if I received my want and not my need
What if I had just the water and not the seed
What if I had the car and not the gas
What if I was always first and not the last

I would lose out on the greatest gift
The weight overwhelming and no way to lift
But if we look past our wants and focus on our need
The lives we could change and mouths we could feed

Learn to have patience in time we must wait
Have faith in God's work hold not onto hate
We will not reap if we don't sow the seed
Plant it in the kingdom you will harvest great indeed

What if every person sowed seed in the faith
This world would be different this world would be great
We must find the need that should be filled
God will supply everything that he has willed

We must take a step forward on the mission
We will see through his eyes and see what is his vision
Sow your seed in the kingdom when you have a dream
You will reap an award you are now on God's team

# What If

What if there was no tomorrow
What if you lost everything
What if you couldn't hear anymore
You lost your voice to sing

What if when you woke up
All your loved ones were gone
What if you lost your mom or dad
Would you be able to go on

Your favorite pet had died
Lost your grandpa to disease
Your grandma passed away
Would this bring you to your knees

We take some things for granted
The food we have to eat
The clothes upon our backs
The shoes that fit our feet

We really are blessed
Blessed to fill our need
More than other people
The little they have to feed

Our children want a car
Or want the latest phone
They want designer clothes
Or a mansion for a home

We should teach them what they have
To others is just a dream
In a second it can be gone
Be grateful for everything

# When You Look

When you look in a mirror
What do you see
A worn-out person who
Is no longer happy

A child who is scared
And filled with fear
Or a weak and timid
Person does appear

Someone out of shape
Someone overweight
Someone who feels
Anything but great

What you see
Is clearly a lie
You are not that person
But a child of the most high

You are a child of a king
A child of the great I am
Do not cower in fear
But in greatness stand

When you look into the mirror
You'll see more clear
The greatness hidden inside
The power standing here

The strength to overcome
The power inside your heart
That today is a new day
Day one of a new start

# Who Is Jesus

He is not just a man
Who lived like the rest
With a regular job
And tries to do best

He is the son of God
A man with no sin
The living peace
We hold within

He walked many miles
To teach those who come
He spoke to the crowds
And the miracles he had done

He taught how to live
And how we should love
He shown them the way
To the father above

Though some were afraid
Of the words that he spoke
He ate with the sinners
The lost and the broke

He told of the events
In the coming of days
The torture he'll feel
And the pain it will raise

He's willing to give
His life up for ours
So we may be forgiven
And to live above the stars

He is Jesus the Christ
Who sits at the right hand
Next to our father
Who created all land

In him I will find
My peace and my joy
In the chosen of time
The evil he'll destroy

On this day I remember
What he gave up for me
So I'll kneel at his cross
Bow my head unto thee